HOW WE
TALK

HOW WE
TALK

The Story of Speech

By

Merilyn Brottman Bennett and Sylvia Sanders

Illustrated by William R. Johnson

Medical Books for Young People

LERNER PUBLICATIONS COMPANY
MINNEAPOLIS, MINNESOTA

CONTENTS

I

Your First Words

You weren't born knowing how to talk. How and when did you learn to speak?

You began practicing the very day of your birth. You didn't, of course, start with words. You began by crying.

As a tiny baby you cried a lot because that was the only way you had to tell people you were hungry, cold, hot, wet, tired or sick. You simply opened your mouth and let out a loud a̲ a̲ a̲ a̲ a̲ a̲ a̲ a̲ sound (as in the word h̲a̲d̲).

Anyone watching could almost see your little muscles tighten as you kicked and screamed. Your voice muscles tightened, too, and caused your cries to become very shrill or high. Much of the sound passed through your nose. It was not a very pretty sound, but it was loud and usually got results.

Sometimes you seemed to cry for no reason at all! You weren't being naughty. You just wanted everyone to know you were happy and satisfied. Crying was your only means of communication and your first step in expressing more than one idea was to develop a second kind of cry.

After you had been fed, or bathed and tucked into a comfortable bed, you were quite content. You made sounds to tell everyone how good you felt. Your muscles were relaxed. Therefore, your cries became lower. They came from your throat instead of your nose. When you opened your mouth to cry, you formed the vowels, oo aw ah o. These sounds were softer and less annoying.

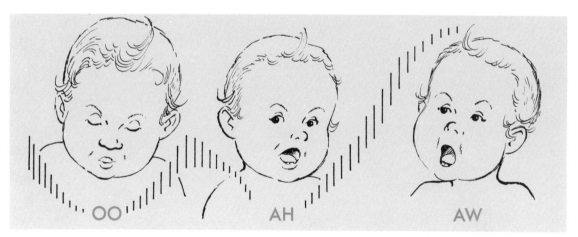

Anyone who spent much time near you soon learned to hear the difference and understand what each of your cries meant.

To make your first cries, you simply opened your mouth and sounded off. Before long, you discovered that you could open and close your mouth while you cried. Now you had three new sounds, the consonants p b m to add to the vowels.

Try saying, <u>pa</u> <u>ba</u> <u>ma</u>. Each of these sounds is made with the same mouth movements. Your tongue is flat inside your mouth and your lips open and close in a natural position. What makes the sounds different from each other? Try them again, and you will find that only your breath is used for the <u>p</u> sound. To change the sound to <u>b</u> you must add voice. By sending the voice up through your nose, you will make the sound of <u>m</u>.

Pretend you are sucking a piece of ice. Where is your tongue? It is against the front of the roof of your mouth. This is where a baby must place his tongue to drink his milk. Sometimes if you were hungry when you cried, you put your tongue in that position. The consonants you made were <u>t</u> <u>d</u> or <u>n</u>.

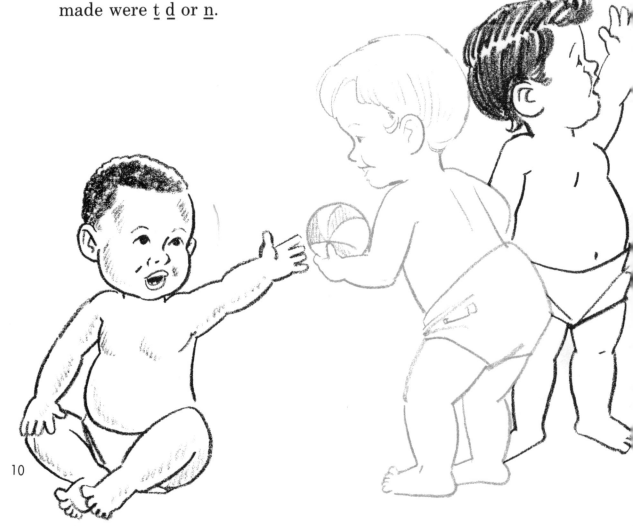

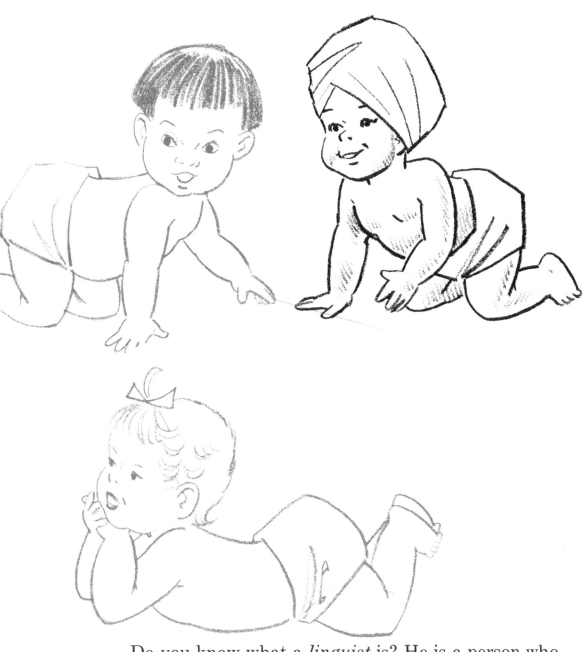

Do you know what a *linguist* is? He is a person who speaks several different languages. You were something of a linguist when you were only four months old! At that age you made every sound used in all human languages. Did you realize that babies from all countries sound the same, before they learn to talk like their parents?

There is a story about an American couple who enrolled in a French speaking class. When asked why they wanted to learn to speak French, they said, "We are going to adopt a French baby girl and we want to be able to understand her when she begins to speak." Let's find out why this is a funny story.

Shortly after four months of age, a baby begins noticing and imitating the sounds he hears. Little by little he discovers which sounds people use more than others. He practices these sounds over and over again.

He is so busy practicing the sounds he hears that he stops using those he does not hear in the language spoken around him. Alas, the baby is no longer a linguist. And the French baby girl will speak whatever language her new parents choose to speak—and without even a trace of a French accent!

Listening is very important in learning to speak. The baby who cannot hear will not be able to learn speech in the same easy way that the average child does.

While you were busy imitating the sounds you heard, your family often imitated what you said. If you happened to accidentally say "ma ma ma" when your mother was around, she may have laughed or smiled and said, "Yes baby, here's mama." You saw she was pleased so you said "ma ma ma" again.

Finally you were no longer accidentally saying "mamama," but you said it when you wanted your mother. Now your sounds were meaningful speech or words.

Did we say you were no longer a linguist? Well, perhaps, in a way you still were. Babies speak their first words at about nine months of age. All over the world those first words are the same: papa, baba, mama, and tata, dada, nana. Do you recognize your first consonants?

Each word may not have the same meaning in every country or even in every home. "Nana" may mean "grandma" in one place, "nurse" in another or "night-night" somewhere else. Since these are always baby's first words, each language has put them to use. You might ask your parents what these words meant to you.

When you were two years old, listening was still very important. You learned the meaning of many words. You heard them spoken many times before you tried saying them yourself. At three you began to use more words. Suddenly you had almost a thousand words in your speech vocabulary. Of course, you didn't say all of these words perfectly. You might have said "twain" for train, or "sanks" for thanks. You probably were seven or eight years old before you used all the speech sounds correctly.

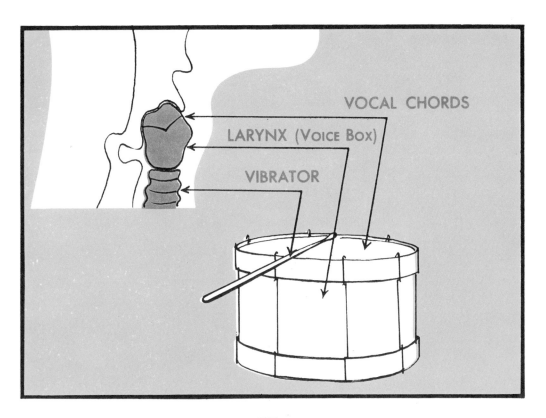

VOCAL CHORDS

LARYNX (Voice Box)

VIBRATOR

II

Your Voice Is Like a Musical Instrument

We discovered how sounds become meaningful words. But how are sounds themselves made? How was it possible for you, as a tiny new baby, to make a crying sound?

Your voice is very much like a musical instrument. Do you know how musical instruments work?

Let's think about a drum. The top or head of a drum is made of animal skin or plastic which is pulled tight. When you beat a drum the drum head *vibrates*. Sound waves bounce around inside the drum. By putting your hands on the top or sides of the drum you can feel the vibrations. The larger the drum, the lower and louder the sound.

You may have a toy or real guitar, banjo or violin.
When you run your fingers across the strings they vibrate.
If you look closely you can see them moving. The short,
thin strings on a small banjo or violin make a high sound
which isn't too loud because the box part of the instrument is small. A large guitar or a big bass violin has much
more room for sound waves to crash around. Its strings
are much longer and thicker, too, so it makes a louder,
lower, booming sound.

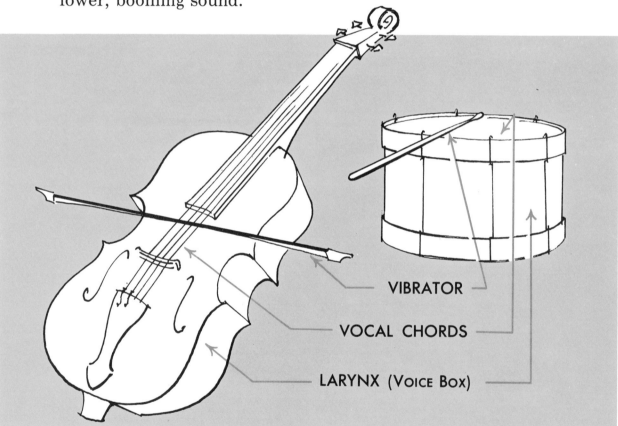

VIBRATOR

VOCAL CHORDS

LARYNX (Voice Box)

Every musical instrument needs three things to make
it work. A part to vibrate, in order to produce sound
waves, something to start the vibrations and a container
of some sort for the sound waves to hit against so they
will become louder.

Our voices are like string instruments. Vocal cords in the throat are stretched across the voice box or *larynx* (LAIR inks). Touch the front of your neck and you will feel a small bulge which is part of the larynx. Sometimes this bulge is quite noticeable in grown men and is called the *Adam's Apple*.

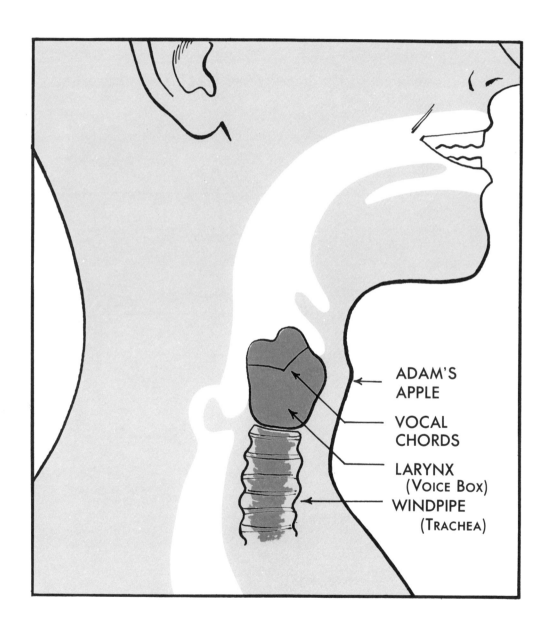

ADAM'S
APPLE

VOCAL
CHORDS

LARYNX
(Voice Box)
WINDPIPE
(Trachea)

We start the vocal cords vibrating with our breath. The larynx, mouth, throat and nose are the containers which increase the volume of the sound. Of course, we don't make a sound with every breath we take. Why?

Musicians usually loosen the strings of their instruments when they are going to put them away. You may have seen them tighten the strings again before they start to play. In much the same way, with ordinary breathing, your vocal cords are loose and relaxed. In order to make a sound, the muscles in the larynx must tighten the cords.

A baby is born knowing how to use his voice instrument. He needs no lessons and he enjoys practicing.

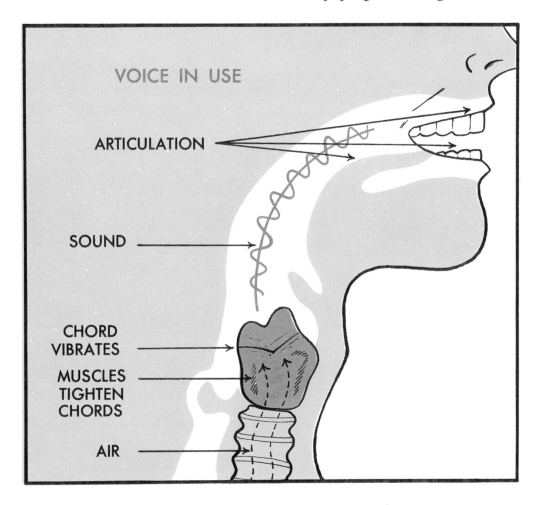

VOICE IN USE

ARTICULATION

SOUND

CHORD VIBRATES

MUSCLES TIGHTEN CHORDS

AIR

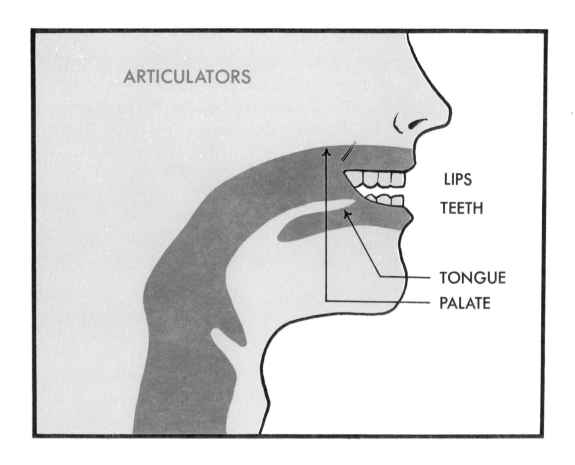

ARTICULATORS

LIPS

TEETH

TONGUE

PALATE

III
Why Can't a Musical Instrument Talk?

A musical instrument produces sound in much the same way that people do. Why, then, can't a musical instrument talk?

We have something special that musical instruments do not have. We have *articulators* (ar TIK you lay tors), which form sounds into words. The tongue, teeth, lips and *palate* (PAL it) are used as articulators. The palate is the roof of your mouth. The front part is hard, the back part is soft.

Ask a friend to help you try this experiment. Have him say, <u>oo</u> <u>aw</u> <u>ah</u> <u>ee</u>. Did you see how he had to change his mouth to form each of these vowels? Now let's try some consonants. Have your friend say these words, <u>bell</u>, <u>shell</u>, <u>fell</u>. Notice how the lips, tongue and teeth move differently for each word?

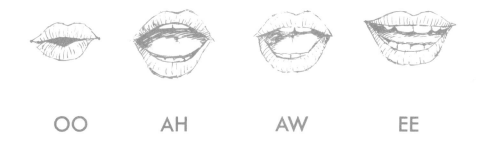

OO   AH   AW   EE

People who are deaf or very hard of hearing cannot hear speech, but they are able to understand what is said by watching three of the articulators. The movements of the lips, tongue and teeth make it possible for the deaf person to see what is spoken. This is called lip reading or speech reading. You might try doing the same thing by turning off the sound on your television. Perhaps you will understand a phrase or two. Certainly you will notice that some people use these three articulators more than others.

When people don't make proper use of their articulators, we say they mumble. Mumblers are very annoying because they are hard to understand. Have you ever heard someone say, "He talks as if he had a mouth full of mush"? What he really means is that the person is not articulating clearly.

There is one kind of person who articulates with his lips as little as possible and does it on purpose. In fact, he practices and practices speaking in this way until he can do it without being a mumbler. He is a *ventriloquist*. He speaks without using his lips and at the same time moves the mouth of a dummy or puppet. To an audience it appears that the dummy or puppet is speaking. A ventriloquist usually has his lips open to let the sound out of his mouth. He keeps his teeth closed to hide the movements of his tongue. He is actually using three of his articulators.

It is much easier to speak, and to be understood, when we use all of our articulators properly.

IV
Why Don't All Voices Sound the Same?

Have you ever played a game where you were blindfolded and had to guess the names of the other players? Or been to a costume party where everyone wore face masks and you had to guess who each person was?

In each of these games, the best clue for guessing correctly is to hear the person speak. Why is this true? Why don't all voices sound the same?

Pitch, intensity, quality and *rate* make each person's speech a little different from everyone else's. Let's begin with *pitch*.

You have heard the high pitch of a small violin with short, thin strings, and the very low pitch of a base fiddle with its large box and long thick strings. The pitch of a voice also depends upon the size of the larynx and the length and thickness of the vocal cords.

Very young boys and girls have small voice boxes. Their voices have a high pitch. As they grow, their voice boxes and vocal cords grow too and their voices gradually lower in pitch.

During the early teens, a boy's voice box and vocal cords suddenly grow much larger and his voice changes. His voice may be high one moment, then suddenly drop to a lower pitch only to go right back up again. The voice finally begins to stay at the lower pitch more and more regularly. From then on, boys have a deeper or lower pitched voice than girls. Girls' voices do not change as much or as suddenly as boys.

The *intensity* (strength) of a voice depends upon the force with which the air strikes the vocal cords. Some voices are loud and strong, others are soft and weak. You may have noticed this about your own classmates when they give oral reports. Some pupils can easily be heard by everyone. Others have difficulty speaking loudly enough for those in the back of the room to hear them. We should talk loud enough to be understood, but not so loud as to annoy people.

Good posture and good breathing habits are necessary for proper voice intensity. Actors, and people who must do a great deal of public speaking, often take special training to increase the intensity of their voices.

Voice *quality* may be clear, pleasant, harsh, irritating, nasal or throaty. Some entertainers have extremely harsh voices. Are you familiar with the cartoon characters, Popeye and his girl friend Olive Oil? Popeye's voice has a throaty quality, while Olive's is high and shrill.

Sometimes the natural quality of a voice changes temporarily. Have you noticed that when someone has a cold and his nose is stopped up, his voice sounds different? If you cheer too hard and long at a basketball game your larynx may become irritated. You will develop a hoarse voice. You may have no voice at all for a short time.

Some people speak so rapidly that they can hardly be understood. They seem to talk "a mile a minute" all the time. Others speak so slowly that sometimes we wish they would speed up a bit. The *rate* of speech is important. It is best to speak slowly enough to be understood, but quickly enough to keep people interested in listening. About 140 words a minute is a good rate of speech for conversation.

There are many times when your normal rate of speech will change. When you must speak to a large group of people it is better if you talk slowly. Unfortunately, this isn't always easy. Have you ever practiced

giving a two minute speech at home and then found at school you got through the whole thing in one minute? Standing in front of the class made you nervous or excited and you increased your rate of speech.

Ordinarily you do speak slower when you are very serious or when you are sad. An explanation of how you broke the neighbor's window would probably be given at a much slower rate than telling how your team won a baseball game.

Have you ever heard yourself talk as others hear you? You hear your speech from the inside of your body as well as from your outer ears. You sound different to other people than you do to yourself. It is an interesting experience to listen to one's own voice on a tape recorder. Your voice may sound strange to you. You may find out it has a different pitch, intensity, quality and rate than you thought.

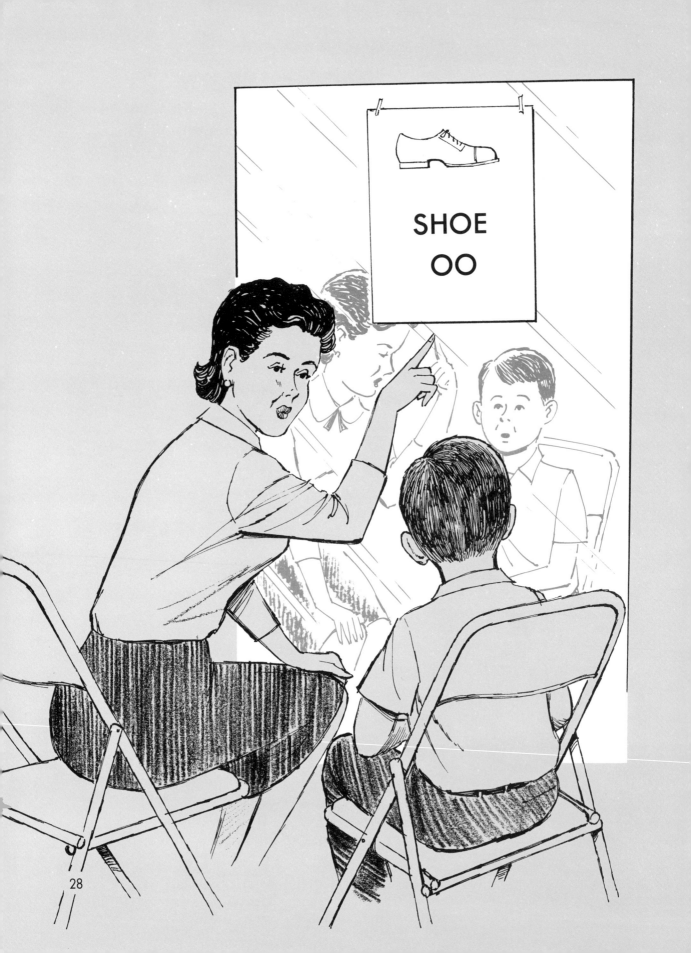

SHOE

OO

V
What Are "Speech Problems"?

A *speech therapist* is a special teacher trained to help people who have speech problems. What are "speech problems"?

Perhaps there is someone in your school who says "Wittle Wed Widing Hood" instead of "Little Red Riding Hood." Or, perhaps you know someone who lisps. A child who lisps would probably say, "Thally ith tho thilly," instead of "Sally is so silly." In both of these cases the children use an improper sound in place of the correct one. The speech therapist can help these children.

Another problem is stuttering. A stutterer keeps repeating the same sound when speaking. The cartoon character Porky the Pig is a good example. At the end of each cartoon he says "Th th that's all f f folks."

Many little children <u>seem</u> to stutter for a short time when they are learning to talk. They think faster than they can speak. The words just won't come quickly enough. As their speech, vocabulary and language improves, they usually outgrow this habit. However, stuttering sometimes continues after a child has been in school for several years, or doesn't start until he is already in school. In these cases the children should not be left to outgrow their poor speech. They have a problem which needs the help of a speech therapist.

Speech therapists work in many different ways to help children with speech problems. One way is to practice sounds in front of a mirror. The child tries to imitate the way the teacher makes the sounds.

We mentioned before that listening is a very important part of learning to speak. A child who is hard of hearing during the years he is learning to talk doesn't hear all of the sounds correctly. Naturally, he pronounces words as he hears them, and thinks he is saying them properly. The speech therapist can help show him the difference between the way he hears words and the way he must say them.

Sometimes a baby is born with a *cleft* (or opening) in the roof of the mouth or upper lip, or with an opening in both of these places. These are called *cleft palate* or *cleft lip*. When this happens, the doctor must operate to close the opening.

Ordinarily you can't see a repaired cleft palate, but you will notice the person's unusual speech. He seems to send all of his breath and voice through his nose.

A repaired cleft lip is more noticeable. There will be a small scar which runs from the upper lip to the nose. Children with repaired cleft palate or cleft lip almost always need help in speech.

Stories, dramatics and games are often used to make the lessons more interesting. For example, if a child doesn't give the s sound properly, the teacher may ask him to hiss like a snake—"s s s s s." If r is the sound the pupil is working on, the teacher may have him try to crow like a rooster—"er er er er."

Hard work goes into the half hour of speech class. Perhaps the hardest of all is for the student to remember to correct his speech at all times. This means not only in speech class, but also in regular school, at home and at play.

VI
Your Speech Tells Where You Live

Supposing three people born in the United States said, "Good Morning" in these different ways:

Good mAW ning

Good mAW nin

Good mAW er ning

Could you guess which person lived in the East, the South and the Midwest?

The native language or *Mother Tongue* of the United States is American English. People in various parts of this country speak it differently.

The early American colonists did not all speak English in exactly the same way. The first settlers to arrive on the eastern coast of America came from southern England. They spoke with a broad a. It is much the same sound you make when the doctor asks you to say "ah ."

Using the "ah" sound, read this sentence aloud: Ask him if he passed her half a mile up the path.

The first settlers did some interesting things with the r sound. If an r followed an a they just skipped the r. Using the "ah" sound again, read this sentence as if there were no r's in it.

He parked the car.
(He pAH kt the cAH)

When the r came at the end of a word, an "uh" sound was used.

MothUH (Mother) and FathUH (Father) came ovUH (over) on the MayflowUH (Mayflower).

Probably most interesting of all, they sometimes used the r where it didn't belong! They often added it to words ending in aw or a.

draw	drawr
Florida	Florider
idea	idear

The people who live in the New England states today still use the speech brought over by the people from southern England.

Those first settlers on the East coast later began moving to the Southern part of this country. Here they also used the broad <u>a</u> and forgot many <u>r</u> sounds. Then little by little they changed their speech.

"Y'all, come again, y'hear."

The people in the South left endings off of some words. "Good mAW ning" became "Good mAW nin." They also began speaking with a drawl. They stretched vowel sounds. It makes the speech of people from the South slower than that of people from the East. Sometimes Southerners stretched the vowels so far, they had room to add another sound. Often a <u>y</u> or <u>w</u> slipped in where it didn't belong. Not long ago a lady from the state of Virginia moved to Iowa. She asked her new friends if they wanted to play "kee yahdz." Her friends said they didn't know how, but would be glad to learn. Imagine their surprise when they found the Southern lady meant "cards"!

Quite a different kind of speech arrived when people from the northern part of England began to settle in the western and northern parts of this country. There was no neglect of the r sound. It was pronounced whenever it appeared in a word. The broad a was used only in a few places: He pah er kt the kah er.

(parked)   (car)

Most of the time they used the short a as in the word "cat." How different this sentence sounds using the short a: Ask him if he passed her half a mile up the path.

We call this kind of speech *General American*. It is spoken by most of the people in the United States today, and especially by those who live in the Midwest. General American speech includes the western drawl we associate with cowboys. However, the speech used by radio and television announcers is most typical of General American speech.

These are the three *main* kinds of speech in the United States. *Eastern, Southern* and *General American*. This doesn't mean that all Eastern speech is the same. The people in New York City do not speak exactly like the people in Philadelphia or Boston. In fact, the speech of people living in one part of New York City may sound quite different from that of people living in another part of the city.

Southern accents may vary too. The people in Norfolk, Virginia speak with an accent different from those who live in Atlanta, Georgia or Miami, Florida.

Even General American speech has differences, though perhaps not as many as the other two main kinds of speech. Of the three main kinds of speech, only General American has spread into all areas.

Because listening and imitating are such important parts of the way we talk, our speech changes when we move from one part of the country to another. A family who moves from the South to the North gradually loses its Southern accent, while one who moves from the North to the South begins to develop a Southern accent. In both cases, children usually change their speech more quickly than their parents.

Is there someone in your school who transferred from another part of the country? Listen and see if you can hear any differences between his speech and yours.

GREEK   SPANISH   RUSSIAN   ARABIC   SIAMESE   KOREAN

There are 2,796 different languages. Not all languages use the same sounds.

We have 26 letters in our alphabet, but we use about 42 sounds in American English speech. Does this seem impossible?

Let's look at this sentence and see how many different sounds the letter o has. "Look, the odd snake is coming to coil on the rope." We can count seven sounds for one letter.

We have about twenty vowel and twenty-two consonant sounds. The Spanish language has only five vowel sounds and the Hawaiian language has only seven consonant sounds. Can you see why it is easier for us to learn to pronounce their words than it is for the Spanish and Hawaiian speaking people to learn to pronounce ours?

We already know how to make most of the sounds in those languages. The people speaking Hawaiian and Spanish have many new sounds to learn when they try to speak American English. We have this same difficulty in learning to pronounce Russian words because that language has many sounds not found in ours.

As a baby you made all of the many different sounds used in every language. Gradually you dropped those you didn't hear and kept only the ones used in the language or languages spoken around you.

When a family with a small child moves to a country where another language is spoken, an interesting thing happens. The child learns two languages at the same time. He usually speaks both languages equally well. You see, he still knows how to make all of the sounds he needs for both languages.

The parents will speak the new language with an accent. They have kept only the sounds needed in their native language. Now they must use the sounds of one language while speaking another.

A person speaking with a German accent says, "Vell, I vouldn't vonder," instead of "Well, I wouldn't wonder." He does this because in the German language a <u>w</u> is pronounced like our <u>v</u> sound. We mustn't laugh at this kind of mistake. We probably wouldn't do much better if we tried to say, "Es macht nichts aus" which means, "it doesn't matter." We haven't had any practice making the German "ch" sound which is not at all like our "ch" but more like our <u>h</u> or <u>k</u>.

When you study a foreign language you may meet up with sounds not used in your native tongue. At first you will probably speak with an accent. But because you are young, your speech organs are still easy to manage. You should, with practice, soon be able to correctly master the new sounds.

Hello   Hallo   ¡Oigo!   Werda?   Allô allô

38

Information
for Parents and Teachers

Parents play an important part in guiding their children toward good speech. Few are aware that they can begin by encouraging baby's cooing and babbling. The more practice the baby has in making every sound there is, the less likely he is to have difficulty later with some particular sound. His articulators will be more flexible and manageable, making it easier for him to correctly imitate the sounds he hears.

A child just beginning to talk should not be expected to say his words perfectly. This takes time and practice, and again the parents can help. Refrain from interrupting, over criticizing or laughing at awkward attempts to utter new words. Offer encouragement by being a good listener and allowing the child time to say what he has to say. Most important, provide him with good examples of speech to imitate.

Resist the temptation to hang on to "cute" mispronunciations. "Pasgetti" for spaghetti, or "frigid rater" for refrigerator are admittedly amusing versions of difficult words. Unfortunately, children are too often encouraged to continue this type of baby talk. When adults imitate a young child's imperfect speech, the child has little to gain. The adults must, without nagging, provide the correct pronunciations.

A normal child's speech development follows the pattern described within this book. It is, however, most important to remember that the age at which a child enters each stage may vary.

It is true that a mentally slow child seldom learns to speak at an early age. However, the normal or bright child may also be late in speaking. Home environment is an influential element in determining this matter.

A second child will very often begin speaking at a later age than the first child, and continue for some time to develop his vocabulary at a slower rate. The first child has usually received undivided adult attention not given to a younger sibling. The second born has the older child to supply and express his needs and wants for him. Twins or children very close in age, have been known to establish their own language, if left to themselves too much of the time.

Problems may sometimes arise in speech development despite excellent parental guidance and good speech patterns in the home environment. There may, for example, be organic difficulties that escape early detection. It is most important that professional help be consulted during the child's early years. In this way it can be determined whether the problem is a minor one, to be ignored and outgrown, or whether therapy is recommended.

Teachers should encourage oral communication in the classroom. Reading aloud, class discussions and dramatics provide exercises in developing good speech habits. Classes of almost any age find listening to their own voice on a tape recorder both fascinating and enlightening.

A teacher should, of course, be on the lookout for students with speech problems and refer these children to the school speech therapist. The teacher should also listen to her own speech. Is she providing a pleasant voice to listen to and a good example of speech to imitate?

Good speech, which has always been an asset, is becoming more and more vital. The telephone, dictaphone, intercom and tape recorder are just a few of the modern-day devices which put emphasis on pleasant, understandable speech.

The authors hope the young readers of this book will gain, (1) an understanding of how we learn to talk, (2) an appreciation of good speech, and (3) a healthy tolerance for those whose speech is in any way "different."

Merilyn B. Bennett received her academic training at the University of Wisconsin. Her degree is in Special Education with a major in Speech Therapy. She subsequently taught in public schools and clinical training programs, and has been awarded a Special Honor Certificate in Clinical Excellence. For the last several years her work has been with deaf and hard-of-hearing children at the Minneapolis Hearing Society, and with hospital patients deprived of speech through illness. Mrs. Bennett is a member of the American Speech and Hearing Association. At present she is a Speech Therapist in the Birmingham Public School System, Birmingham, Michigan.

Sylvia Sanders trained to be a teacher for the deaf. She earned a B.S. degree from South Dakota State College and an M.A. degree from Gallaudet College in Washington, D.C. She has taught in schools for the deaf in South Dakota, Maryland and Pennsylvania. When Mr. Sanders was in the Navy, Mrs. Sanders tutored privately all the way from California to Virginia. She is a member of the Minnesota Author's Guild and has published numerous stories and articles. The Sanders family, which includes two teenage daughters, resides in Minneapolis. Mrs. Sanders now works primarily with preschool hearing impaired children at the Minneapolis Hearing Society.

This photograph shows Mrs. Sanders tutoring a girl before a mirror.

STEINBERG STUDIO

William R. Johnson is a book illustrator, commercial artist and cartoonist. He is the author-illustrator of "Holiday Funtime," and draws the weekly sports cartoon "Letter From the Twins" appearing in the St. Paul Dispatch. In 1964 he was the recipient of an Honor Award from the Freedom Foundation at Valley Forge for an editorial cartoon. Mr. Johnson and his family reside in Coon Rapids, Minnesota.